Special educational needs policy options steering group

Rethinking Support for More Inclusive Schooling

POLICY PAPER 1
(third series)

Contents

Edited by Brahm Norwich.

SPECIAL EDUCATIONAL NEEDS

POLICY OPTIONS STEERING GROUP

POLICY PAPER 1
(third series)

Rethinking Support for More
Inclusive Schooling

A NASEN PUBLICATION

ISBN 1 901485 04 8

Published by NASEN.
NASEN is a company limited by guarantee, registered in England and Wales. Company No. 2674379.
NASEN is a registered charity. Charity No. 1007023.

Further copies of this book and details of NASEN's many other publications may be obtained from the Publications Department at its registered office: NASEN House, 4/5, Amber Business Village, Amber Close, Amington, Tamworth, Staffs. B77 4RP.
Tel: 01827 311500; Fax: 01827 313005
Email: welcome@nasen.org.uk
Web site: www.nasen.org.uk

Cover design by Graphic Images.
Typeset in Times by J. C. Typesetting and printed in the United Kingdom by Stowes.

Chapter 1
Introduction to Policy Paper

This paper is a record of the recent Policy Seminar held at the Institute of Education, London University (November 1998) which examined the question of RETHINKING SUPPORT FOR MORE INCLUSIVE SCHOOLING. It was the first seminar in the third round of these SEN Policy Option Seminar series. The aim of the seminar was to consider issues and new initiatives relevant to support systems and their contribution to more inclusive schooling. The Steering Group decided to focus on support issues following the publication of the SEN Action Plan and the Government's commitment to inclusion. Our rationale was that more inclusion means greater demands on schools and therefore the need for closer and more immediate support from internal and external support services.

There were contributions from a wide range of perspectives. The Steering Group decided to invite representatives from LEAs, special educational needs co-ordinators (SENCOs), external support services and the voluntary sector. Clive Danks, Advisor for Birmingham LEA, introduced the seminar in terms of current policy initiatives following the Green Paper and SEN Action Plan. Peter Gray, an SEN Policy Consultant presented a perspective on policy issues relevant to support systems. This was followed by Barbara Burke, Assistant Director of Education, talking about support in Newham LEA. Jeff Franks, an SEN Team Manager from Hillingdon, talked about joint social services and education department links in his area. The role and work of the SENCO was described by Ruth Newbury, SENCO from Sandy, Bedfordshire. The Educational Psychology Service perspective was analysed by Rik Boxer, Principal Educational Psychologist in Luton LEA. Joan Baxter, from the Place to Be, a voluntary support organisation, outlined the perspective and work of her organisation. The themes from small group discussions are summarised at the end of the paper.

About 50 people participated in the day seminar, coming from schools, LEA support services, LEA officers, Government Agencies (DfEE and OFSTED), parent groups, the voluntary sector, health service professionals, educational psychologists and universities.

SEN Policy Options Steering Group
Background

This policy paper is the first one in the third series of seminars and conferences to be organised by the SEN POLICY OPTIONS STEERING GROUP. This group organised the initial ESRC-Cadbury Trust series on policy options for special educational needs in the 1990s. This first series led to the second one which was supported financially by NASEN. (See the list of these policy papers published by NASEN at the end of this section.) The Steering Group has representatives from LEA administrators, head teachers, voluntary organisations, professional associations, universities and research. Given the success of the first and second series of policy seminars and papers, a further round of seminars and conferences in this field has been organised with further funding from NASEN. These events are intended to consider current and future policy issues in the field in a proactive way. They are planned to interest all those concerned with policy matters in special educational needs.

Aims and objectives of the Policy Options Group

1. to identify current and likely future policy problems and the options for solutions in special education provision following the Green Paper 1997 through to the year 2000 and beyond;

2. to organise conferences and seminars for policy-makers, professionals, parents, voluntary associations and researchers in the field and publish the proceedings for wider dissemination;

3. to enhance the two-way relationship between policy and service issues and research agendas.

Current Steering Group membership
     Mr Keith Bovair, Head teacher Durrants School (NASEN representative); Mr Clive Danks, Advisor, Birmingham LEA; Mr Tony Dessent, Director of Education, Luton LEA; Dr Seamus Hegarty, Director of the National Foundation for Educational Research; Professor Geoff Lindsay, Warwick University; Dr Ingrid Lunt, Reader, Institute of Education, London University; Mr Vincent McDonnell, Director of Education, Richmond LEA, Mr Chris Marshall (OFSTED); Professor Brahm Norwich, Institute of Education, London University; Mrs Margaret Peter; Mrs Philippa Russell, Director of Council for Disabled Children; Professor Klaus Wedell, Institute of Education, London University.

Current series
     The current series aims to organise four full or half day events on special education policy and provision over the two years 1998/99-1999/2000

which are relevant to the context of considerable changes in the education system.

If you have any ideas about possible topics or would like to know more about the events, please do contact a member of the Group or Brahm Norwich at 25 Woburn Square, London WC1H 0AA.

Policy Options Papers from first seminar series published and available from NASEN

1. Bucking the Market: LEAs and Special Needs
Peter Housden, Chief Education Officer, Nottinghamshire LEA.

2. Towards Effective Schools for All
Mel Ainscow, Cambridge University Institute of Education.

3. Teacher Education for Special Educational Needs
Professor Peter Mittler, Manchester University.

4. Allocating Resources for SEN Provision
Jennifer Evans and Ingrid Lunt, Institute of Education, London University.

5. Planning and Diversity: Special schools and their Alternatives
Max Hunt, Director of Education, Stockport LEA.

6. Options for Partnership between Health, Education and Social Services
Tony Dessent, Senior Assistant Director, Nottinghamshire LEA.

7. Provision for Special Educational Needs from the Perspectives of Service Users
Micheline Mason, Robina Mallet, Colin Low and Philippa Russell.

Policy Options Papers from second seminar series published and available from NASEN

1. Independence and Interdependence? Responsibilities for SEN in the Unitary and County Authorities
Roy Atkinson, Michael Peters, Derek Jones, Simon Gardner and Philippa Russell.

2. Inclusion or Exclusion: Future Policy for Emotional and Behavioural Difficulties
John Bangs, Peter Gray and Greg Richardson.

3. Baseline Assessment: Benefits and Pitfalls
Geoff Lindsay, Max Hunt, Sheila Wolfendale and Peter Tymms.

4. Future policy for SEN: Responding to the Green Paper
Brahm Norwich, Ann Lewis, John Moore and Harry Daniels.

Chapter 2
1. Policy issues raised by rethinking support

PETER GRAY, SEN Policy Consultant

Introduction

Let us assume we all thought that inclusion was a good idea. What impact might this have on the way schools were organised? Would there be a continuing need for external support services or for any specialist provision?

The reality of course is that the path to successful inclusion is a **process** rather than something that can happen overnight. However, the Green Paper is signalling greater Government expectations about progress in that direction than has perhaps been the case previously. How does support need to be rethought to help achieve this?

Need for clear objectives

There has been much debate about the meaning of 'inclusive schooling', with concerns being raised about whether locational integration is a sufficient criterion. The consequence of this is that there is some confusion about how successful support for inclusion might be measured. For example, are units in mainstream schools a good thing (even if pupils are fully included), if in fact they are catering for pupils who might previously have been supported in their own local school? Is it a good thing to have a growing number of Statemented pupils in mainstream schools, if numbers in special school provision are not decreasing at similar levels?

While qualitative measures of inclusion are important, quantitative indicators (eg the percentage of pupils entering special provision) also need to be used. However, there is not much clear evidence at present that use is made of *either* kind of measure when evaluating the outcomes of support or when considering its focus.

Corporate vision

This lack of objectives and performance measures is sometimes compounded by the different emphases and priorities of support providers. For example, in focusing on reducing pupil exclusions, some Behaviour Support teams can contribute to greater demand for special school placements. Without a corporate vision for inclusive schooling, across schools and support agencies, there is a real risk of unintentional (even sometimes intentional) sabotage.

Conflicting agendas

Providers of support to mainstream schools often encounter some resistance to notions of inclusion, particularly in relation to pupils with challenging behaviour. Mainstream access for many pupils with significant special educational needs is dependent on schools receiving additional resources from the LEA. There can be conflicts even here about the levels of resourcing that schools and support providers consider to be appropriate.

Support for inclusive schooling needs to take this on board. At the individual pupil level, it will be necessary to work through the resistance and pessimism that is often encountered and to show what is possible. Successful support should be directed at achieving mainstream ownership of the pupil, but without an over-dependence on outside resources to achieve this (as ultimately this is unsustainable).

At the policy level, continual debate is necessary with elected members, other officers, support service managers and schools to highlight the rationale for inclusion and the costs, as well as benefits, of segregated provision.

Needless to say, managing such conflicts of value and interest require considerable resilience, both for those working in schools and those offering support from outside.

'Enskilling'

Support for inclusive schooling requires an ability and commitment to 'enskill' those who normally have responsibility for educating pupils (class teachers and parents). There are still too many examples of people feeling deskilled and less confident as a result of support worker involvement.

Support therefore needs to be capable of making teaching methods and approaches accessible to 'ordinary teachers', parents and learning support assistants rather than restricting knowledge and skills to a small number of specialists.

Support: internal or external?

The pressure on LEAs to delegate expenditure to schools has inevitably reduced the extent of support available to schools from outside. Some would argue that this is a *good* thing and that the retention of any significant external support does not help progress towards mainstream schools owning responsibility for children with special educational needs. The Government's latest document on school finance ('Fair Funding') implies that LEAs should only retain specialist support for low-incidence types of need (eg sensory), with any other external support being purchased by schools as necessary.

In a fully inclusive situation, where mainstream schools own total responsibility for providing a quality education for *all* pupils, it is probably appropriate to delegate as much as possible, and to develop more local systems of support within schools to ensure needs are met. However, the reality is not like that. The LEA currently retains the legal duty to ensure pupils' needs are met and they have had little power over recent years to dictate school priorities when individuals' needs have been at risk. In the case of pupils with emotional and behavioural difficulties, schools are within their rights to exclude pupils and LEAs are increasingly being expected to make alternative provision.

In this context, unless there is stronger commitment at school level to include, LEAs have no choice but to retain reasonable levels of external support to help ensure mainstream access for pupils where this is seen to be at risk.

It is however still possible to enhance inclusive schooling by co-ordinating both internal and external support at 'cluster' level.

Focusing our energies

There have been exhortations for greater inclusion on previous occasions, before the Green Paper. How can support workers make a real difference this time?

I would argue that the key task is to divide our time effectively between two priorities: 1) achieving whole school development and 2) focusing our individual pupil support on those children with the most severe and complex needs. It may still be appropriate to develop schools through joint work with individual pupils or groups, but we need to judge the effectiveness of such inputs at a whole school level (in terms of longer-term skill transfer or curriculum/system adjustments).

Supporting individual pupils with more challenging needs is often a difficult task and may require the development of new skills for all those involved in support, in schools and outside. It may also require better support and supervision opportunities for support providers. External services can sometimes fulfil this role for in-school staff, drawing on wider experiences. However, local SENCO networks and other problem-solving groups can also be very useful. Support services themselves will also need effective and supportive supervision structures.

Final comments

There are many current barriers to the development of more inclusive schooling. Support services often point to inflexibility in LEA resourcing approaches and lack of clear inclusive policies at national and local level, as examples of these. Even in this context, however, there is still much that can be achieved, provided that those involved in supporting pupils and schools share an inclusive focus and are clear about their support objectives. Making genuine progress, however, can be hard and requires a mutually supportive ethos, both between school-based staff and external services and within support services themselves.

2. Some current policy issues: Meeting Special Educational Needs - A Programme for Action

CLIVE DANKS, Advisor, Birmingham LEA

The Government in its recently published *Meeting Special Educational Needs: A Programme for Action*, has made an unequivocal statement on the fully inclusive society, accepting the fundamental case for 'inclusive education' and providing as far as possible for special needs in mainstream schools.

A Programme for Action is wide ranging in its proposals but none more so than in Chapter Three: Moving towards Inclusive Education. Critical to the debate on inclusion, and putting current thought into context, is a vision of a local inclusive education network and not simply isolated 'inclusive' schools.

This fundamental statement goes beyond the notion of a basic continuum of organisational options for meeting pupils with SEN set out by Cope and Anderson (1977) and offered as a model by Hunt (1994) in *Planning and Diversity: Special Schools and their Alternatives*, to a new and more complex structure. It is one in which a number of schools (including special), along with support services, provide a 'basket of provision' that is broad enough to meet a wide and ever-changing range of local individual needs.

The broader debate

Whilst in practice this is a model that I can support, it needs to be set in the context of a wider debate. Education is grappling with Fair Funding, Behaviour Support Plans, Educational Development Plans, Target Setting and the Literacy Strategy. In Health and Social Services, their respective White Papers, and most recently Partnerships in Action (New Opportunities for Joint Working between Health and Social Services), have also raised a whole new agenda.

In creating an inclusive ethos, the Government places that responsibility jointly on LEAs and schools to work in partnership. Unfortunately for the beleaguered SEN officer, this is a task that will become increasingly more complex with the 'fallout' from Educational Development Plans and Fair Funding and the shift to new funding mechanisms under the Standards Fund. And, this is before speaking with colleagues in Health and Social Services regarding 'non-educational provision'. I do not think there has ever been a time when the term 'joined up thinking' has been more appropriate.

Whilst setting aside the fundamental structural and financial change about to impact on LEAs, Dessent (1996) argued that: 'Multi-agency work is bedevilled by the development of a plethora of cross-agency groups with unclear remits which are poorly connected to each other.' His logical conclusion was to formalise inter-agency structures and processes for collaborative work at three levels: policy and strategic planning, neighbourhood/area planning and individual pupil/families, so that we may offer a way through the moral maze of inclusion.

If we accept his three 'elements', then it is essential that support services be represented at all stages in the process, and not just supporting the individual pupil.

Currently, Birmingham is embarking on a wide consultation programme: *Towards Inclusion* (1998) involving all stakeholders. In order to take the debate forwards, the LEA has established a cross-services strategic planning group incorporating both senior managers and service providers, in a total overhaul of SEN provision.

Funding local authority support services

Under the new Fair Funding/Education Development Plan (EDP) structure, LEAs must now be accountable and totally transparent for centrally maintained funding. Many authorities may be faced with the position of delegating some service funding and even with slight movements, service managers may see a significant shift in their capability to deliver a 'corporate' service for the LEA. This is at a time of greater expectations for mainstream schools to provide inclusive societies. The alternative argument is that the process of delegation through Fair Funding can effectively absolve schools of SEN probity, whilst leaving the locus of responsibility, as defined under the 1996 Act, with the LEA.

Clearly then, as the effects of Fair Funding/EDP unfold, it will be of paramount importance that both the quality and quantity of individual services reaching the child in the class are maintained, either through local or national monitoring.

Role of special schools and support services

As we move into the next millennium, the role of special schools will significantly change in the 'inclusive society'. Here, the traditional role of segregated provision must fall away as more pupils attend their local mainstream school. This will necessitate a closer tripartite relationship with mainstream schools and support services in offering a flexible and corporate 'education service'. For some services and schools, this will be a new venture requiring sensitive management in the first few years.

Co-terminosity

So far, I have concentrated on local authority services. However, for many of the children and young people, it is often access to Health and Social Services that eventually determines the level of inclusion possible. For this reason, I strongly believe we need to look at co-terminosity of all services in small local networks. The establishment of the Primary Health Care areas can assist local authorities in mapping out their own services for pupils with SEN, especially if a local authority is reorganising current provision.

Provision

Currently under section 322 of the Education Act (1996), the LEA has ultimate responsibility for securing provision under Part III of a Statement of SEN ('educational provision'), unless the child's parents have made appropriate alternative arrangements. Consequently, some LEAs purchase provision directly from NHS Trusts, others have joint commissioning, whilst in many authorities there are tensions between Health and Education about who will pay for therapy for particular children. As a result, there is a need to revisit section 28a of the NHS Act (1977), in the light of providing integrated services.

The DfEE working group, established to review the inter-relationship, is most welcome. For example, funding clarity across the Government's Sure Start Programme will enable a closer liaison between all providers in a co-ordinated and targeted approach, and reaching those children and families for whom access to support services in the past has been patchy, fragmented or non-existent.

Regional planning

The Green Paper states that LEAs and other interests need to work effectively together on a regional basis, particularly for low incidence disabilities. Currently, there are five DfEE pilot studies considering the arrangements for co-ordinating provision. In these authorities, current support services may take on a wider role. The 'research' evidence from the pilots could form the basis for long-term provision for all LEAs.

Parents

Over 3,600 consultation responses were received from the Green Paper; over a quarter of these were from parents and pupils. The SEN Action Programme spells out the crucial role parents and carers play in their child's education and clearly, the inter-relationship between parents/carers, pupils' schools and support services is critical. This is particularly true for 'children looked-after', the role of Social Services as carer, and the move towards inclusive school societies. The reaffirmation of the importance of parent partnership schemes and a broadening of dialogue at all stages, will have significant implications for all services.

'Service structure' may benefit from designating staff with specific responsibility for contact with parents; others may consider 'single point of contact'. Whatever approach is adopted, the 'public face' of the service will, for some, be the critical indicator of effectiveness in spite of the efficient operation of the rest of the service.

Staff training

Finally, in what is currently a wide-ranging set of developments, the training of staff at all levels will be crucial. The Government in the SEN Action Programme highlighted new opportunities in the Standards Fund. Circular 13/98 clarifies the position. If authorities, Education, Social and Health, are to move forward on inclusion, the opportunity for specific and generic training across all services is of vital importance.

Concluding comments: two perspectives

Special education is at a junction. For the first time in many years, there is both a drive from central government and a willingness from teachers, support staff, therapists and parents to work more closely for the purpose of educating pupils with SEN in a more inclusive system. Clearly, this places a significant pressure on officers and managers to revisit current structures and practice in order to meet these new requirements. If we get the thinking, planning, funding and delivery 'joined up', then the services provided to children and young people can only improve and become more effective in ensuring the greatest level of opportunity for inclusion. If, for any reason, managers are not able to 'close the circle', then we may be faced with further fragmentation of services, lack of co-ordination and failed expectations for those young people we wish to support. Critical to the whole debate, are the strategic planning processes, effective liaison and co-ordinated delivery of services from all providers.

References

Birmingham LEA (1998) *Towards Inclusion* (Unpublished discussion paper in a series Achieving in Partnership). Birmingham LEA.

Cope, C. and Anderson, E. (1977) *Special Units in Ordinary Schools.* Windsor: NFER.

Department for Education and Employment (1998) *Meeting Special Educational Needs: A Programme for Action.* London: HMSO.

Department for Education and Employment (1997) *Excellence for All Children: Meeting Special Educational Needs.* London: HMSO.

Department for Education and Employment (1998) *Circular 13/98: The Standards Fund 1998.* London: HMSO.

Dessent, T. (1996) *Options for Partnership between Health, Education and Social Services.* Tamworth: NASEN.

Hunt, M. (1994) *Planning and Diversity: Special Schools and their Alternatives.* Tamworth: NASEN.

3. LEA Support Services: A Newham Perspective

BARBARA BURKE, Assistant Director, Newham LEA

Support services in Newham

Over the past ten years, support services in the London Borough of Newham have been characterised by growth.

At the present time there are six support services in the borough:

Learning Support Service,
Behaviour Support and Tuition Service, including the PRU,
Service for Deaf and Partially Hearing Children,
Service for the Visually Impaired,
Home and Hospital Tuition Service,
Language and Communication Support Service.

In 1987, there were approximately 30 members of staff. The services now employ over 250 staff of whom 120 are teachers and 130 learning support assistants. This expansion has necessitated major changes in both organisation and management style. Informal lines of communication have had to be replaced by more structured systems. Service Level Agreements have been negotiated with schools. The increasing success of inclusion in Newham schools and the difficulties in effectively managing a provision of this size have led to the devolving of some of the funding and responsibility to schools. Since September 1996 the provision for pupils with non-complex learning difficulties at secondary level has been directly managed by schools. Certainly, now that inclusive education has become widely accepted in Newham it has become increasingly possible to devolve or delegate funds for SEN support to mainstream schools. This has been done in the secure knowledge that schools will continue to support an inclusive approach.

Inclusion

In Newham over 90% of pupils with Statements of Special Educational Needs are educated in mainstream schools. In 1986 Newham Council adopted a policy of integrating pupils with special educational needs into mainstream schools. As special schools closed, pupils were educated in either their local mainstream school with support, or placed in a mainstream school with a resourced provision. Currently, there are two special schools in Newham and there are plans to amalgamate these into one. There are 86 pupils educated in these schools and 85 pupils are educated in out-of-borough special schools.

The mission statement on inclusive education states the following:

The ultimate goal of Newham's Inclusive Education policy is to make it possible for every child, whatever special educational needs they may have, to attend their neighbourhood school, and to have full access to the National Curriculum and to be able to participate in every aspect of mainstream life and achieve their full potential.

The role of the support services

It is difficult to be precise as to the varying roles that support services perform; this is because perceptions as to their role vary according to the user of the service. Schools, for example, may well have a very different set of expectations from parents. Perhaps, support services perform three key roles although the distinctions between them are somewhat arbitrary and frequently overlap.

The prime purpose of most support services is to enable schools to fulfil their statutory duty towards **individual pupils**. In Newham, support is provided primarily to pupils who have gone through the stages of the Code of Practice and have a Statement of Special Educational Needs. Both teachers and learning support assistants provide direct support to pupils. Support staff, working in this way, deal with issues of access and differentiation within a National Curriculum that can appear narrow and academic. Part of their role is to ensure that teachers in schools are aware of the importance of identifying and providing for those pupils who have special educational needs. More recently support staff have been at the forefront in including pupils with special educational needs in the Literacy and Numeracy hours. At times, this role becomes that of advocate for pupils who are always in a minority in a mainstream setting and in danger of being marginalised. Support service staff work to ensure that pupils with special educational needs are included in all the activities of the school that are open to their age group.

Moving away from a focus on individual support to that of school level support, services have a key role in school improvement. At a time when schools are judged in terms of examinations, SATs results and league tables, the issue of **school improvement** becomes one of vital concern. Support services frequently hold key information on adapting tasks and tests, special examination arrangements and alternative accreditation for pupils whose achievements are not recognised at Grade G at GCSE. Such information can enable pupils with special educational needs to demonstrate just what they can achieve. The advantages of such information are two-fold. Firstly, disapplications can be minimised and secondly, some pupils with special educational needs can demonstrate their part in school improvement. In terms of behaviour support, school improvement can be shown by the number of pupils at risk of exclusion being maintained in school and achieving exam success. Increasingly support staff have been involved in working with and 'skilling up' SENCOs following the increasing demands made of them by the *Code of Practice*. On a wider level, support services can be directly involved in reinforcing LEA policies and in working with schools to develop whole school policies.

The third role of support services, and one which is particularly important in an inclusive setting, is that of retaining a team of specialists to provide **advice and training**. In Newham, specialist teams include teachers of autism, specific learning difficulty, severe learning difficulty and information technology. All these teams have a responsibility to keep up to date with national developments in special educational needs.

In addition to supporting pupils these teachers offer training and advice across the borough for teachers, governors and parents. Currently seven in-service training courses, accredited by the Institute of Education, are offered to Newham teachers:

Table 1 - In-Service Training Courses

Title	Maximum No. of Participants	Pattern of Delivery	Responsibility for Delivery
SENCO Training (Double Module)	20	10 days	Learning Support Service
Severe Learning Difficulties (Double Module)	10	10 days	Learning Support Service
Language and Communication	20	18 twilights	Language and Communication
ICT in the Inclusive Setting	10	2 days 8 twilights	Learning Support Service
Autism in the Ordinary School	10	2 days 8 twilights	Specialist teachers of autism
Visual Impairment & Multiple Disabilities	10	2 days 8 twilights	Visually Impaired Service
Positive Behaviour	20	18 twilights	Behaviour Support and Tuition Service

The Learning Support Service also currently trains 60 learning support assistants a year on a City and Guilds course. Staff who successfully complete the course are automatically promoted. The role of the support assistant is particularly complex and such training is vital if assistants are to move away from simply acting as 'minders'.

Service effectiveness

One of the key questions that has to be answered is that of how service effectiveness can be measured. Most support services have a variety of ways of monitoring staff effectiveness. For example, record keeping, planning, written reports and a consideration of the appropriateness of differentiated targets and approaches can all be examined. It is more difficult to measure how well a support teacher is managing to work collaboratively with a class teacher, how ideas are exchanged and to what extent the support teacher manages to leave the class teacher skilled and valued. Similarly, it is difficult to find ways of measuring effectiveness that can form the basis of comparison not only within an LEA but also between LEAs.

Cost indicators

In terms of cost it is possible to calculate the cost of support to a pupil in relation both to the number of pupils in the borough and to the number of pupils supported.

Table 2 - Support Service Cost Indicators

Service	School Population (P)	Supported Pupils (S)	Service Budget (B)	Cost Indicator to School Population B/P	Cost Indicator related to supported pupils B/S
Learning Support	45,070	595	£4,139,616	£91.85	£6,957
Behaviour Support and Tuition	16,013*	236	£1,276,457	£79.71	£5,409
Visually Impaired	45,070	163	£298,415	£6.60	£1,831
Deaf and Partially Hearing	45,070	290	£314,008	£6.95	£1,083
Language and Communication	45,070	40	£112,673	£2.50	£2,817
Hospital and Home Tuition	45,070	664	£297,173	£6.59	£447.55

* Secondary school population

21

Contact indicators

These, too, can give an indication of the level of contact services have in relation to the number of pupils in the borough.

Table 3 - Support Service Contact Indicators

Service	School Population (P)	Supported Pupils (S)	Contact Indicator S/Px100
Learning Support	45,070	595	1.32%
Behaviour Support and Tuition	16,013*	236	1.47%
Visually Impaired	45,070	163	0.36%
Deaf and Partially Hearing	45,070	290	0.6%
Language and Communication	45,070	40	0.09%
Hospital and Home Tuition	45,070	664	1.5%

* Secondary school population

Performance indicators

Traditionally, support services have been wary of using performance indicators. Where they have been most comfortable has been in monitoring individual pupil progress. The targets achieved in any Individual Action Plan provide a useful guide at annual review for those pupils who have a Statement of Special Educational Needs. On a wider level, SATs and examination results for pupils can give an indication of progress, particularly in terms of value added. In Newham, exam results have risen year by year and exclusions have fallen overall since the introduction of inclusion. Finally, services can be evaluated through monitoring the comments made in Ofsted reports as well as through feedback from schools, pupils and parents.

The future

i) Fair Funding

In its consultation paper *Fair Funding: Improving Delegation to Schools* the Government sets out its proposals for increasing financial delegation to LEAs. These proposals replace and develop the current regulations for local management of schools (LMS). This new system, known as Devolved Funding, takes effect from April 1999. At first sight, the implications for support services would appear to be limited, as special educational provision is one of four key areas that LEAs can choose to retain centrally. Certainly, the responsibility to produce Statements of Special Educational Needs and to ensure that pupils receive the provision specified in Statements rests with LEAs and not with governing bodies. This, as the consultation paper states, 'creates a presumption in favour of retaining a major proportion of the necessary funds centrally' (Paragraph 27). The paper states that any approach should be based on consultation and consensus with schools. In Newham, the view is that greater delegation of funding enables schools to take on the responsibility to include pupils with special educational needs. However, there is also recognition that this needs to be balanced by retaining centrally a strong core of staff who can offer specialist advice and expertise.

Perhaps of greater significance to support services is the issue of Value for Money. Services need to demonstrate that they are effective in schools and that mechanisms are in place for monitoring and evaluation. Support services in Newham are currently being reviewed under Best Value. This is a fundamental review of the way that all services, which support the requirements of pupils with SEN, are organised.

ii) Inclusive Practice

The Green Paper provides a welcome boost to the development of inclusion but remains fairly neutral with regard to support services. The assumption that 'teachers in special schools are uniquely equipped to help their colleagues in mainstream' is simplistic. Whilst there are many highly skilled individuals in special schools, not all of them are able or willing to progress inclusion in mainstream schools. If current special school practices are directly transferred to a mainstream setting there is a danger that teaching and learning styles are adopted which might isolate pupils with special educational needs. Although the Green Paper does not acknowledge it, support services have a vital role in bridging and adapting special school practices to make them work for teachers in the mainstream classroom.

Support services in Newham are currently working to make the theory of inclusion meaningful. In the past year, a Charter and Audit on Inclusion has been produced. Parents, teachers and other professionals developed the Charter. Over 95% of schools have adopted the Charter through their governing bodies and have used it to celebrate and monitor their inclusive education practice. The Audit was designed to be a working document to help schools identify their own priorities in developing Inclusive Education. It provides schools with examples of good practice based on research carried out in Newham schools. In September, guidance on

'Including Pupils with Special Educational Needs in the Literacy Hour' was issued to schools. Support services are uniquely placed to assist schools in their difficult task of balancing a focus on individual pupils with special educational needs with that of the wider issues of whole school effectiveness.

4. Joint initiatives - Education and Social Services

JEFF FRANK, SEN Team Manager, Hillingdon LEA

Background

This paper is written from the perspective of a middle manager in Hillingdon, with responsibility for ensuring that children with special educational needs have those needs appropriately met. I bring to the post 12 years experience within Social Services, together with seven years as a practitioner in both mainstream and special schools. It is my belief that joint working is not only desirable but also essential if we are to offer an effective service to young people.

This paper is split into six sections and outlines the experience of joint - working between the local education authority (LEA) and the Social Services Department (SSD) in a number of key areas pertaining to special needs.

The recently published DfEE Programme of Action reinforces the importance of inclusion in mainstream schools. For local authorities this can present a dilemma when seeking placement for pupils returning to the borough from expensive specialist resources. It is not always possible for them to be placed directly into local mainstream schools. This points the way to a new role for day special schools, in supporting such placements.

Driving forces encouraging joint agency working

There are a number of driving forces that give impetus to joint working between education and social services at a national level. Multi-agency Children Plans have been a significant influence across the country in establishing joint agency working. The networking opportunities in Hillingdon have meant that it has been possible to identify the key players in a position to move initiatives forward.

In addition, LEAs are currently producing Behaviour Support Plans and a high degree of inter-agency consultation has been required. A number of the recommendations arising from the plan have implications for further joint working. The commitment to 'Best Value' is another important factor that serves to encourage joint working.

To summarise, some of the national influences on this area of work include:

- Children Plans

- Green Paper

- Best Value

- Behaviour Support Plans

- Initiatives for Looked-after Children

Why inter-agency working?

From a pragmatic standpoint, joint working makes sense. Financially, it is possible to maximise limited resources. A planned and co-operative approach is to be encouraged. Further, agencies do not find themselves working against each other and are less likely to be manipulated. It is easier to achieve a degree of consistency for children. A time-consuming case-by-case approach can be avoided, which often results in inconsistent decisions being taken.

Perhaps most important, service can be centred on need, rather than agency requirements. A proactive style can be adopted, to the benefit of children. Outcome focus takes an increased precedence over sector priorities.

Joint working in Hillingdon

First of all, it was necessary to identify common areas of concern:

1. the need for a planned approach towards supporting preschool children

2. the prohibitive cost of out-borough placements

3. the recognised advantages of joint working at the transition stage.

The process adopted was to start by agreeing common areas of concern. Procedures were then discussed and agreed. Next came endorsement through respective Education and Social Services Committees. Throughout the entire process openness between all parties was essential. Both parties then agreed the following criteria:

- clarity of purpose and a clearly co-ordinated approach

- identification of realistic objectives

- focus on success: specific targets and goals

- named representatives attend meetings, with the authority to make decisions that have funding implications

- built-in review.

The Hillingdon Experience to date
The experience has been a very positive one and has established a structure for further joint working in the future. To date, the joint working between the LEA and the SSD has created a positive atmosphere of co-operation and has resulted in an enhanced spirit of collaboration. Currently there are three initiatives/projects in operation:

Joint Planning and Funding Panel
This joint initiative has now been functioning for just under a year in its current form. It is an inter-agency panel that represents the Special Educational Needs section of the Education Department and the Children and Families Department of Social Services. A joint working protocol was agreed by both departments and then endorsed by the respective committees. The brief is to make joint decisions on out-borough placements and to closely monitor young people already jointly funded. This panel has now been extended to include representation from the Health Authority in the person of the Health Policy Adviser.

Preschool Co-ordinating Group
The purpose of this established group is to ensure that there is a well co-ordinated approach in Hillingdon for preschoolers who may have special educational needs. This group involves Health agency staff as well as SSD staff. It has been successful in ensuring that appropriate provision is made for children. The exchange of information amongst agencies has proved to be invaluable over the two years that it has been functioning in its current form.

Joint Transition Planning Group
This group, now under the auspices of the Social Services, is in effect the combination of two separate groups, to ensure that there is a seamless service available in Hillingdon for young people who are about to leave full-time education. The Careers service is also represented in this group.

The three initiatives are seen as successful and are valued. Improved practice has resulted and there is an atmosphere of co-operation and partnership. One agency can only have a limited impact.

Future development
The principle of inclusion is central to the Green Paper and the implications of a policy of increased inclusion within mainstream schools are considerable for both LEAs and Social Services Departments. As the latter seek to find

more local provision, so there will be increased pressure on both mainstream and day special schools to take more pupils who would have been placed in out-borough provision in the past. The Green Paper recognises this and suggests a redefinition of the role of special schools. This has considerable implications for the role of Social Workers.

However, the most effective means of increasing inclusion is to avoid the exclusion of pupils from schools in the first place. The whole issue of children out of school would benefit from a joint approach and is an area where there is room for further development. Increased involvement of the SSD is likely to result in preventative work, so reducing the number of pupils excluded from our schools. (The statutory duty of the SSD in this respect is outlined in the 1989 Children Act.)

Joint training initiatives for both SSD and LEA staff are currently under consideration, with the intention of further developing the understanding of each other's role. (In the joint placements protocol there is a clear commitment to developing this initiative.)

Although not part of the local authority, it is recognised that the Health Authority has a crucial part to play if we are to ensure the delivery of effective, improved and appropriate services for children.

Further development of current initiatives is envisaged as the systems that have been established are dynamic in nature. One possible development of the Joint Placement and Funding panel will be for a shared pool of money to resource the panel's decisions. In addition, it is envisaged that the monitoring role of the panel will increase as time goes on.

A paradigm shift is required, away from a fire-fighting model, towards a long-term planned approach. Short-term, reactive responses tend to be ineffectual (too little, too late) and expensive. Joint working, if approached correctly, can encourage a move towards proactive, appropriate, effective and financially sound working practices.

It has recently been said that 'joined up problems require joined up solutions' (Quoted in *'Findings'*, Joseph Rowntree Foundation, October 1998).

A concerted effort is required if we are to make the moves forward that are necessary. Perhaps even at a national level a 'Children's Department' is necessary in order to co-ordinate inter-agency policies. The intention must be to bring about sustainable change. In other words, to give rise to improved service delivery for young people with special needs. That is why we have a duty to implement this approach.

5. The role of the SENCO

RUTH NEWBURY, Sandy Upper School, Bedfordshire

Inclusive education reflects the true comprehensive ideal. Schools should be places that provide for all students, but inclusion will be an uncomfortable and unrewarding place without the real desire to provide what is necessary for all students.

Inclusive education is currently a two-level process. It is about access to the whole curriculum for all students within a school. It is also about the role of the special school and where those students, who are currently educated within that area, fit into the whole spectrum of inclusive education.

Special Needs/Learning Support provision is fundamental to the style of the school. It is central to what the school is. It is not a bolt on part, added when the rest of the provision is in place. The school ethos – demonstrating commitment to all – is required if inclusion is to be successful for all areas of student development – both social and academic.

As a SENCO, I want to provide the appropriate learning environment for every student in my school's catchment area, together with those who opt to attend our school.

Therefore, it is not just lip-service that needs to be paid to inclusive education. It is a resource implication that demands space, time, money and staff.

All SENCOs will operate within systems that have a variety of constraints – and we have to operate within those systems – regardless of whether they are appropriate for our students.

Funding

In my authority, a Statement equals money that comes in addition to the school budget. In a neighbouring authority, Special Needs money is allocated to the school on a per capita basis. I run a budget of between £50,000-£60,000 ostensibly for the needs of students holding a Statement, but I am also able to support a number of other students from this budget, as I juggle my time-tabled provision. A colleague in the neighbouring authority functions with a budget of £250,000 for the whole school provision.

Another authority's solution is to suggest that 99% of the budget goes to a School's Forum where group decision as to student support will be made.

I am well aware, via the SENCO Forum, of colleagues who attempt to provide a whole school response from a general departmental allowance of under £1,000 a year. Appropriate provision must be able to be made within each school for all students, rather than the level of funding being determined by a differing rationale dependent on the locality of the school.

Without the correct level of funding, operating under a fair system that will guarantee equality of opportunities for these students, integration will be achieved by paying only lip service to the principles required.

Resources

The need for the right materials for each student is paramount, together with the right tools to enable them to demonstrate their learning. I still spend a considerable amount of time searching for materials designed for aphasic students, for example. I consider a key feature of learning to involve the development of skills such as keyboarding. Computers, maintained with the right programmes and enough disc space, are expensive. I need voice recognition systems.

More adaptable teaching resources are needed than are currently published. Text invariably has to be altered for a number of students. I would welcome publishing via CD-ROM/computer programmes, and being able to buy the text and teaching resources publications where they can be fed into the computer – font size altered, graphs and pictures enlarged, and text edited by rewording or highlighting subject-specific vocabulary.

ILPs (Successmaker, Global and other programmes designed for specific learning needs) answer many of the individual learning programme needs. However, they have resourcing implications again; the best are extremely expensive.

Staffing

There are training implications for all staff (particularly for those with only the one-year PGCE), for considerations of SEN of a general nature. There will also always be the need for the very specific inputs required when those with the rarer types of disability enter the school.

I have seven other staff in my department – a mixture of full and part time – and I also use Non-Teaching Assistants (NTAs) for a large proportion of the in-class support, for a very specific reason. Where understanding is paramount, I prefer to provide in-class support with a person who has minimal knowledge in that subject. If our NTAs have difficulty in understanding the lesson, my students have little hope of real learning taking place.

A greater use of NTAs needs to be explored – together with the extension of accredited courses at extended levels. Currently, NTA training comes to a stop after NVQ Advanced level and I seek courses that will enable my staff to have recognised qualifications that reflect their skills and expertise, in both dealing with specific resources and with students.

I also employ a member of staff as a counsellor. I can only afford her for four hours a week and I could use her full time. The use of counselling and being able to place students with a regular mentor has paid dividends. Far fewer incidents come from those students who are lucky enough to have their initial problems recognised, and appropriate solutions explored and finally put in place, before real problems have arisen. In a world where inadequacies in students' lives outside school have a real impact on the quality of their learning, this service appears to be a growth area, and one that deserves serious consideration to be part of the provision required in schools.

Local authority support services

I want to be able to consult other professionals who are necessary for my students, the same way as I can consult my GP! If it is a real emergency, staff can be made instantly available – otherwise appointments can be made within a realistic time scale.

It is a year since I have been able to meet with an Educational Psychologist – and then only because I had to see him regarding the need for GCSE special arrangements for the current year. The time to discuss general topics reflecting the current intake, for example, does not exist. Speech therapists, support and advisory staff carry heavy loads.

Levels of staffing for these posts, where expert practitioners are required for advice to schools, are woefully inadequate. Appointments are prioritised to those students undergoing the Statementing process at Stage 4, and even then, there are authorities unable to fulfil their obligations as to time scale required by the *Code of Practice*. This is a particularly crucial area in the EBD field – where preventative measures taken early on may obviate the need for later provision.

The *Code of Practice*/local authority procedures

In schools where good practice is part and parcel of its functioning, it is not always appropriate to have to consult with an outside agency at Stage 3. To be given advice which merely reiterates and extends what has been happening at Stage 1 or 2, or is indeed part and parcel of general pastoral procedures, does little to improve the lot of many students and may indeed lead to exclusion rather than to support the student.

There are a number of constraints that hamper the delivery of inclusive education within the mainstream school.

The National Curriculum

The requirements of the National Curriculum fill the mainstream school day. Invariably, time needs to be made to enable staff to address the individual needs of specific students. Choices have to be made regarding the fulfilling of the legal requirements of the Statement, covering the spectrum of the National Curriculum, and providing for the child's needs as seen on a day-to-day basis.

Disapplication has been a lengthy process. The ability for a school to be able to alter the provision at KS4 is a welcome change.

The Literacy Hour

A basic level of literacy for all students is a clear aim with current Government thinking. Why is the Literacy Hour only for the primary sector? Many of my colleagues in the secondary sector of education and I would welcome a time allocation to address basic literacy needs on a mandatory basis rather than having to juggle the current curriculum. Why an hour? Why all in one go? Why class teaching?

The league tables

Whilst these are in existence in their current form, many schools will be dissuaded from implementing inclusive education.

Within a one form entry primary school, one child with significant learning needs may make a difference of up to 4% in the league table statistics. Primary schools are already seeking not to have more than one such child in each year group. At the other end of the spectrum, those students who can perform at levels above those offered for their year group, will also not be reflected in the school's results. The league tables are published in the popular press, generally without informed comment and, in their current form, they work to the detriment of both schools and students.

School architecture

Currently, the school I work in can provide for a variety of need. We have partially sighted, deaf, a variety of specific needs students, students with general learning difficulties and those with behavioural concerns (an ever-growing number). Although our school is a purpose built Upper School (which can cater for over 1,000 students), we have severe problems of access for physically handicapped students. It is tower block, with specialist department areas on upper floors and currently no lift – although we could see where we could put one – losing three department offices and a main entrance in the process. We also have entrances with steps and swing doors everywhere, together with a passage that about 800 children cross at each lesson change, where just about three people may walk abreast. Worktop heights, wheelchair access through all our doors and other basic provision are further considerations. Making our school into an appropriate environment for all students who live within its catchment area would become a very expensive undertaking.

Concluding comments

I would love to think that:

- all students could be catered for within their local catchment area as of right;

- resources would follow a child and not the child the resources;

- parents, teachers and child could all work in partnership with each other and that we could make decisions that reflected need rather than seeking to comply with current regulations;

- the *Code of Practice* did not drown us in paper;

- administration did not get in the way of teaching.

To be able to educate all students in an effective and appropriate manner needs more than is provided at the moment. Life is inclusive! And we are educating our students for life!

6. Educational Psychology Service perspective

RIK BOXER, Principal Educational Psychologist, Luton LEA

Introduction

I am very pleased to have the opportunity to contribute to this seminar. In Luton, as a newly created unitary authority with a commitment to developing inclusive approaches, we are going through the process of reappraising the support we give to schools and the role of support services. I have been asked to talk from an Educational Psychology Service perspective but I would like to start by setting out some of the broader issues for the LEA.

The LEA context

In order to move effectively towards inclusive schooling, work needs to go on at many different levels.

I would argue that the following are key issues.

1. The establishment of a clear policy framework, through a consultation process with all concerned parties, which sets out policy objectives which are commonly understood and measurable.

2. As part of the overall policy framework, it is essential to develop a coherent resourcing policy. Experience in Luton, and elsewhere, shows that it is possible to move away from a model of predominantly individual resourcing through statutory processes. The alternative model is based on whole-school resourcing, whereby schools are resourced to take account of predictable variations in individual needs amongst their pupils. Only children with the most exceptional needs would be subject to statutory assessment. A 'low-Statementing' policy of this sort, although not a panacea, is consistent with inclusive practice and opens up opportunities for refocusing the work of support services.

3. The development of a culture of collaborative working between the LEA, school, parents and relevant agencies and also amongst LEA services to ensure the different 'arms' of the service are working together towards common objectives. Careful attention needs to be given to the development of service organisation and structures which promote collaboration.

4. An exploration of the values and principles underpinning inclusion so that there is engagement with people's hopes, fears and beliefs in order to establish a climate which encourages shifting perceptions of 'What should be' and 'What can be'.

Rethinking the work of support services needs to be undertaken within the context of an overall strategy for inclusion. However, the work of support services is vital to the success of inclusive approaches. They have a front-line role in translating policy into practice and helping to manage the process of change. In order to effectively fulfil this role, there needs to be a reappraisal of practice and priorities.

Developing a more inclusive model of service delivery

The Green Paper (DfEE, 1977) recognises that a move towards more inclusive approaches will have implications for the work of educational psychologists (EPs). There is reference to the need to 'explore ways of changing the balance of work of EPs' but the nature of the changes required in order to work effectively within an inclusive framework needs to be developed in much greater detail.

I will suggest that there are four major shifts which are associated with a more inclusive model of service delivery:

- Assessment to Intervention

- Expertise to Empowerment

- Reactive to Proactive

- Procedural to Transformational

1. From assessment to intervention

Traditional assessment approaches are based on a deficit model. They are concerned with how a child is functioning in comparison with others of his/her age and in identifying where specific problems lie from a within-child perspective. This is associated with a categorisation of difficulties and provides limited help in determining what next steps may be required. Yet there is some evidence that EPs are returning to the use of psychometric approaches (Lokke et al., 1997) and feel under pressure to undertake 'one-off' assessment as part of the statutory assessment process. This is concerning. It is not an inclusive methodology.

Educational psychologists, and other support services, are often asked to address questions which are separatist in nature (eg How severe are these difficulties? Should he/she really be in this school?) Any inclusive model of service delivery must focus carefully on the questions which are being asked and engage in a process of discussion to attempt to reframe concerns in a more constructive way (eg What arrangements would need to be in place in school to better meet his/her needs? How can he/she be helped to make more friends?)

An alternative to a 'within-child' model is an interactionist model which recognises the impact of contextual factors in influencing a child's learning and development. It is possible to construct an assessment framework which remains concerned with the uniqueness of the individual but also focuses on relevant factors in the wider situation which may require change (Boxer et al., 1991)

This would involve:

a. Gaining a holistic view of the child looking at different dimensions of learning (see Barrs et al., 1990 for further details).

b. Identifying factors in the classroom, school and community contexts which may be relevant to the child's learning and development.

c. Making links and connections and formulating hypotheses.

d. Agreeing, implementing and reviewing interventions.

This is a collaborative model, based on joint problem-solving between the EP, school, parent and child. It places the emphasis on discussion and observation rather than 'testing' and is concerned with finding out what works. It is based on the notion that assessment without intervention is not useful to inclusion.

2. From expertise to empowerment

The whole concept of special educational needs as being the province of the expert has been a significant barrier to inclusion. The role of support services should be to empower and bring about change through developing the confidence of teachers, parents and children.

Good inclusive practice is based on an understanding of how children learn and provides an underpinning methodology for all children. The focus should be on extending and supplementing existing good practice, avoiding highly individualised approaches where possible.

Experts can be popular, but can all too easily transmit a message to teachers and parents that special needs can only be met by special arrangements which ordinary schools cannot be reasonably expected to provide.

A much more challenging role is to develop a service which recognises the issues relating to management of change and is concerned with working with others to support children's needs being met in their local school. It is as much concerned with 'people factors' (Taylor, 1992) as it is with issues of technical expertise.

Support services also have an important role in helping schools to learn from each other and to provide an overview of good practice beyond a particular institution. The development of cluster arrangements (Lunt et al., 1994) can be particularly helpful in promoting collaboration and shared responsibility.

3. From reactive to proactive approaches

The effectiveness of Educational Psychology Services has often been seen in terms of responsiveness to schools. Whilst this is clearly an important consideration, EPs should operate from a wider LEA perspective and take on an active role in priority setting. In developing an inclusive model of service delivery, it is necessary to think carefully about the focus of the work, in terms of the impact which is likely to be made towards inclusion. In the Luton context, we are beginning to look at the implications for service delivery in these terms and have identified the following key areas for EP work:

a. A focus on the most exceptional children who are difficult to include. As well as priority Stage 3 work, this would include work at Stage 4 and Stage 5 of the *Code of Practice*, where detailed planning is likely to be required in order to effectively meet a pupil's needs. There is an emphasis on following through with complex casework and retaining a professional responsibility over time.

b. A consideration of critical times when EP involvement is likely to be helpful, at key transition points (eg preschoolers entering school, primary/secondary transfers, special/mainstream transfers) and where there are particular parental and school concerns.

c. Linking with the social exclusion agenda, a focus on those children who are out of school or not receiving full-time education in order to plan and support their return to school.

d. Support for school-based projects, working with schools to help them develop and implement inclusive approaches.

We are striving to develop a model based on proactive work, working closely with schools, parents and others but within a wider LEA framework which helps to inform priorities.

4. From procedural to transformational

This paper is suggesting that there may need to be a change in the nature of the relationship between SEN support service and schools, with particular attention to finding the appropriate balance of support and challenge. The model of 'appreciative enquiry' (Brighouse, 1998) seems to have a lot to offer.

It involves:

a. Appreciate the best of what is

b. Envision what might be

c. Dialogue for new knowledge and theory - what should be

d. Create the vision - what will be.

EPs work in a legislative framework, which sometimes leads to an over emphasis on procedural aspects. Procedures are important in providing a commonly understood framework, but effective support services should move beyond the procedural to the transformational. Services need to consider what are the key elements in their service delivery, organisation and focus of work which contribute most strongly to bringing about positive change.

Concluding comments

There is no simple blueprint for inclusion. A strong policy framework and coherent resourcing arrangements are not enough in themselves. There needs to be a supported shift in practice which, in turn, is linked to personal commitments and beliefs towards inclusion. It is a shared responsibility.

References

Barrs, M., Ellis, J., Hester, H., Thomas, A. (1990) *Patterns of Learning. The Primary Language Record and the National Curriculum.* Centre of Language in Primary Education.

Boxer, R., Challen, M., and McCarthy, M. (1991) Developing an assessment framework: The distinctive contribution of the educational psychologist. *Educational Psychology in Practice*, 7 (1), 30-35.

Brighouse, T. (1998) Quoted at the Institute of Education Guardian Debate held on 4 March 1998.

Department for Education and Employment (1997) *Excellence for All Children - Meeting Special Educational Needs*. London: HMSO.

Lokke, C., Gersch, I., M'gadzah, H. and Frederickson, N. (1997) The resurrection of psychometrics: fact or fiction? *Educational Psychology in Practice*, 12 (4), 222-233.

Lunt, I., Evans, J., Norwich, B., and Wedell, K. (1994) *Working Together: Inter-school collaboration for special needs*. London: David Fulton Publishers.

Taylor, G. (1992) Integration: Breaking down some of the barriers. *Educational and Child Psychology*, 9 (4).

7. A perspective from a voluntary support agency

JOAN BAXTER, The Place to Be

The Place to Be achieved charitable status in 1994. Its mission is to enable emotional and therapeutic support to be provided to children in schools based on a practical model backed up by research.

Primary schools in Southwark, Lambeth, Camden and Chatham, Kent are currently receiving a range of services which undergo continuous evaluation. Early results already reveal an impact on the behaviour of individual children, the climate of the school, parent, teacher and child perceptions of change, and on measures of exclusion, unauthorised absence and SEN. Results of the one-to-one work with children undertaken during 1997/98 reveal that in 87% of cases teachers reported a good outcome to the therapeutic support.

Measures to assess the clinical impact of interventions on individual children have recently been introduced.

Children's mental health

Mental health problems are relatively common in children. Between 10% and 25% of children nationally may be in need of help at some time and the proportion has been increasing over the past 50 years. In some regions, mental health problems significantly exceed the national figures.

The influential study 'What works for whom?' by Roth and Fonagy (1996) in a review of psychotherapy research came to the following conclusions:

The sequelae of childhood disorders include not just a greatly increased risk of mental disorders in adulthood, but also generally poor adaptation, and thus have implications for adult health service resources and the general wealth-creating capacity of these individuals... The low rate of cases reaching (child) psychiatric services highlights a social problem for this group ... who do not themselves have the resources to seek help. The pattern of referrals ... implies that it is the caregiver's rather than the child's needs that are the determinants of seeking psychiatric care ... there seems to be an urgent need to draw caregivers' attention to the possibility that distressed children under their care may not 'grow out of it' and may require psychological help... The high prevalence of these disorders implies that attention should be focused on the development of intervention programs which can be integrated with educational initiatives and made as accessible as possible.

Statistics on adult mental health reveal that there is no room for complacency. Mental health problems are common and increasing. For example, World Health Organisation statistics suggest that by 2004, depression will be the second-biggest health problem in the world.

Mental health is difficult to define, but for children it is generally accepted to include the following:

- a capacity to enter into and sustain mutually satisfying relationships;

- continuing progression of psychological development;

- an ability to play and to learn so that attainments are appropriate for age and intellectual level;

- a developing moral sense of right and wrong;

- the degree of psychological distress and maladaptive behaviour being within normal limits for the child's age and context (NHS Health Advisory Service 1995).

The overall rates of mental health problems have been shown to vary according to the circumstances and environments in which children live. Factors that increase the risk of mental health problems in children include the following:

Factors that increase the risk of mental health problems in children

---

ENVIRONMENT
Socio-economic disadvantage
Homelessness
Disaster
Discrimination
Other negative life events

FAMILY
Parental conflict
Family breakdown
Inconsistent or ambiguous discipline
Hostile and rejecting relationships
Failure to meet child's developing needs
Abuse – physical, sexual or emotional
Parental mental illness
Parental criminality
Parental alcoholism
Parental personality disorder
Death and loss – including friends

CHILD
Genetic
Low IQ
Learning disability
Academic failure
Specific developmental delay
Communication difficulty
Temperament
Physical illness – esp. chronic and/or neurological
Low self-esteem

Not all of those children who encounter circumstances which predispose them to mental health problems will succumb. A range of factors appears to protect children.

Factors that increase the resilience of young people to mental health problems
Self-esteem Sociability Autonomy Family compassion Family warmth Absence of parental discord Social support systems that encourage personal effort and coping

The aims of prevention and early intervention in support of children's mental health should include action to reduce risk factors as well as the promotion of resilience.

Emotional and behavioural difficulties

Professionals working in the Education Services and Social Services tend to categorise problems and disorders differently from Health professionals. Indeed, one of the significant difficulties in coordinating work between departments appears to stem from a problem of taxonomy. The way in which childhood difficulties are perceived, understood and classified also reflects the limits of responsibility exercised by the various agencies and hence the nature of the support or treatment provided.

Children with mental health problems may be recognised within Education Departments as having *special educational needs* because of a learning difficulty which is associated with an emotional and behavioural difficulty. Within Social Services Departments, such children may be identified as *children in need*. Only if departmentally- led assessments confirm that a child has a special educational need or is in need will additional resources be made available to the child via Education and Social Services Departments respectively.

Not surprisingly, there is little consensus over what constitutes an emotional and behavioural difficulty. Explanations tend to depend on the point of view of the observer. In schools, teacher attributions will determine the actions taken in response to children's behaviour. Research indicates that the acceptability of behaviour depends on the context in which it arises, the attitude of the observer, the gender of the observed, the cause to which the behaviour is attributed.

Within Education, there seems to be some debate about whether children whose behaviour causes concern have psychological problems (need treating), have learning problems (need education/training/modification to relearn how to behave) or are just plain bad and should be segregated/punished. Research has also shown that both teachers and non-teachers view emotional difficulties as less of an issue than behavioural difficulties. However, teachers tend to rate emotional difficulties as significantly less of a problem than do non-teachers.

Where emotional difficulties are not accompanied by a significant learning difficulty, schools seem to be less likely to judge that additional support is warranted from special educational needs resources.

Where academic learning difficulties have not been identified by teachers and children are categorised as having behavioural difficulties only, it is also less likely that a full, multi-agency assessment will be carried out under special educational needs provisions.

Even where such an assessment is carried out, the special educational provision forthcoming is unlikely to address the child's emotional needs directly.

What the majority of teachers are almost certainly unaware of is the strong association between depression and conduct disorder, especially in boys. Conduct disorder, typically defined by a predisposition to disruptive, anti-social behaviour, is often a precursor to alcohol, drug and substance abuse. Recent evidence suggests a strong link between conduct disorder and maternal depression during infancy.

Indeed, it would appear that the accurate identification of emotional difficulties in children and adolescents falls outside the competence of most teachers such that the school-based assessment of children with emotional and behavioural difficulties or with mental health problems is at present unreliable.

Schools have a tendency to locate behavioural difficulties which arise for individual children in school *wholly* within the child and to look to family history and child rearing for explanations. Despite the high proportion of children who exhibit mental health problems year on year, there is a strong body of opinion within the teaching profession that teachers should not be expected to deal with children who experience difficulties with behaviour. The rising rates of exclusion and the pattern of variation in exclusion rates across schools suggest that it is teacher attitudes rather than the incidence or nature of emotional and behavioural difficulties that determine the educational treatment received by pupils in difficulty.

Organisational life itself has a profound effect on individual behaviour. The Elton Report among others recognised that behavioural difficulties in schools arise within situations rather than within individuals. Some of the situations which occur in schools may be experienced as challenging by many pupils. Other situations may significantly challenge only the most vulnerable. How potentially challenging situations are managed by school staff will determine the extent to which pupils with mental health problems are supported.

The learning process may itself provide a particular challenge to pupils who have a history of learning difficulty and who have low self-esteem. The question of whether and to what extent schools themselves, with their primary task of academic achievement, may undermine children's behaviour and indeed mental health has never been satisfactorily explored.

Prevention

The scientific evidence to date strongly supports the case for early intervention and prevention in support of children's mental health. Preventive strategies can now be firmly rooted in research findings to tackle specific risk factors and harness protective factors.

Education in school is a universal service offering a wide range of opportunities for preventive work with young people. Education and experience at school that fosters self-esteem and optimal educational attainment, placing appropriate value on achievements that are not purely academic, will itself promote the psychological well-being and resilience of children.

The importance of prevention has been recognised in the recent DfEE circular *LEA Behaviour Support Plans* in which 'measures aimed at early identification and intervention' should be set out so that 'serious problems can be prevented from developing'.

As long ago as 1989, The Elton Report commented positively on the role of voluntary projects in providing preventive support for children at risk of developing behavioural difficulties. It was a recommendation of that report that 'the Government should evaluate preventive schemes aimed at primary age children with a view to encouraging the development of such schemes if they are found to be effective'.

Prevention programmes have been running in the USA since the 1950s with, by now, a wealth of evidence as to their effectiveness. One such scheme, PMHP, has been operating in various States in the USA since 1957, providing one-to-one play-based social-emotional support for primary aged children who have externalising or internalising problems as well as learning difficulties.

Of particular note is the finding that aggression and other forms of acting out, disruptive behaviour is preventable through early intervention. Another important finding is that programmes which are durable over time tend to be intensive, multi-component, multi-level interventions which target individual, social and organisational factors in schools (Durlak, 1995).

Why The Place To Be exists

The schools in South East London where The Place to Be originated serve populations that are particularly disadvantaged and where a high proportion of children are significantly at risk of developing mental health problems. One estimate suggests that only 25% of the local school population is problem-free. It was the schools' experience that many children in great need were unable to access local mental health provision, this being attributed in part to the unwillingness of parents to use these services. The local Educational Psychology Service was described by headteachers as being chronically short of staff and unable to cope with the volume of cases. The schools went in search of workers who could understand and work with children's emotional difficulties and who were prepared to come into school and see children on site. The outcome was a team of arts therapists, play therapists and counsellors in training or already qualified who saw individual children weekly, worked with groups and in some cases whole classes on a voluntary basis.

Provision

Uniquely, P2B has developed a comprehensive range of services in support of children's emotional needs within the school context, with reference to the existing literature and to our own outcome evaluation. The focus is on prevention, working with primary aged children and avoiding waiting lists. Children may be referred by parents, carers and teachers or may self-refer through The Place to Talk which operates during lunch breaks.

Through a carefully designed Referral and Assessment Process, P2B and school staff identify the appropriate response to individual needs, including referral to external agencies where appropriate.

Direct work with children

- Individual sessions
  - communication through a range of media ... play, art, drama etc. Up to 1 year's duration x 1 per week. Trainees (not first years) closely supervised and line managed by qualified School Project Managers.

46

- Group sessions
  - small groups, weekly for 8 sessions with trained staff

- Place to Talk
  - 1:1 self-referral, trained staff, lunch-breaks

Work with parents

- Initial and follow-up
  - meetings to share information, promote partnership, identify aims

- Referral
  - to relevant agency for personal support if requested

- Solution-focused Brief Therapy
  - joint meetings with SENCOs and School Project Managers

Work with school staff

- INSET
  - induction and follow-up

- Reviews
  - regular casework with teachers and bi-annual reviews with heads

- IEPs
  - sharing responsibility at Stage 3 of *Code of Practice*

- Teacher consultation
  - individual sessions to promote insight, understanding and effective strategies

- Organisational consultancy
  - helping schools to review relevant policy and implement change

- Curriculum
  - working with teachers to develop curricula in support of emotional needs

The ways in which children communicate their emotional needs may present schools and carers with problems of management – both the management of behaviour and the management of feelings. Teachers and schools need support in understanding the feelings and behaviour of the children and their own role in this so that future transactions may be managed helpfully.

The size and scope of P2B projects are tailor-made to meet the wishes and needs of individual schools. Timing is important too in matching what is offered to the developmental needs of the school. Fund-raising, the deployment of trainees and efficiency mean that comprehensive, quality support is provided at low cost.

References

Durlak, J. (1995) *School-based Intervention Programs for Children and Adolescents.* London: Sage Publishers.

NHS Health Advisory Service (1995) *Together we stand: the commissioning role and management of child and adolescent mental health services.* London: HMSO.

Roth, I. and Fonagy, P. (1996) *A Critical Review of Psychotherapy Research.* New York: The Guilford Press.

Chapter 3
Summary of discussion and conclusion

The discussions during the Policy Seminar were in small groups and then finally in a plenary group at the end of the day.

Issues concerned with resourcing and the use of Statements were raised in several groups. The need to have even funding across all LEAs was identified in one group with the proposal that teachers be paid centrally. At a local level there was a recognition that the chase for individual resourcing, based on a tension between parents, schools and LEAs, was a barrier to inclusion and hindered collaborative working. Several participants grappled with the question of how can resources for pupils with significant SEN be more 'upfront' (that is, be available without the need for a Statement) in a way that safeguarded individual needs and promoted effective inclusion. One suggested answer was to give schools more discretion and delegation of funding for these pupils, but this needed to be backed up with strong support services and thorough training. However, the system was portrayed by several participants as focusing too much on the individual child. The *Code of Practice* and more recently the basis for more delegation to schools through Fair Funding was seen to reinforce this individual focus.

On the question of support services for schools, it was pointed out that there had been fragmentation over the last decade in support services. There was a major need, it was asserted, to change the culture in some support services and that this was an enormous job.

On the question of training for more inclusion, preparing teachers in initial teacher training was mentioned by several participants as very important. The preparation and training of parents and non-teaching assistants (NTAs) was also noted in discussions. As regards NTAs, this role was seen as under-used and undervalued. The need for an appropriate career structure for NTAs was highlighted. SEN co-ordinators were also identified as a group which needed more training.

In promoting inclusion several participants referred to the role of LEAs. It was suggested that LEAs should link up their inclusion policies with other initiatives such as Educational Development Plans and Behaviour Support Plans. The importance of involving members of the Education Committees in inclusion and resourcing issues was also noted.

On the question of the organisation of services, it was asked whether there were better ways of promoting local networks. Clusters of schools with delegated funding was seen as one way to give more power to SEN co-ordinators and promote improved support.

The role of schools was seen as crucial in promoting inclusion. Someone asserted that research showed that the best teaching and learning was going on in the most inclusive schools. The source of this research was not provided. However, schools were seen to need help in identifying the numerous practical steps which can be taken to increase inclusion. In response to this, reference was made to models of school review and development which had been and were currently under development, for example, the CSIE/Open University/Manchester University framework, the Newham Audit system and the Birmingham self-review materials. The contribution of external consultancy to support such development reviews was mentioned. So was inspection in opening up issues about maximising potential for all children, the kind of principle often referred to in schools' mission statements. Providing schools with information about children going to special schools and units in their area was found in Nottinghamshire to be a powerful way of communicating to schools about their responsibilities to all children. However, there was a question about whether we have an appropriate system of school governance if we are serious about inclusion. That this is not a simple matter was indicated by another question: how far should schools be responsible for SEN? In relation to this question it was commented that the Code of Practice had eroded school responsibility.

The importance of inter-service collaboration was mentioned by several participants. It was generally accepted that there was a need to consider the responsibilities of Health and Social Services in any inclusion programme. Joint planning and joint funding were praised as an excellent idea. The work in Birmingham between Education, Health and Social Services and Housing mentioned as an example. It was also pointed out that Education services could be brought into the current Partnership in Action initiative. But, Health Trusts have difficult decisions to make about balancing budgets between hospital and community services. One suggestion was that Government could ring fence health budgets for children's services. Another was that strategic planning across services was better with joint management of services.

Some of the discussion focused on current Government educational policies. The SEN Action Plan following the Green Paper was criticised for not giving enough attention to the question of support services to promote inclusion policies. Inclusion policies, it was pointed out, were also subject to influences and general pressures on educational policies.

Three other factors were identified as significant for schools to become more inclusive, first, the issue of children being happy at school and second, parents' need to be kept correctly informed. Otherwise parents will become suspicious and defensive about inclusive practices. The third factor was time. Someone wondered whether schools were becoming more inclusive and asked whether schools can think in the current climate, let alone rethink their SEN support systems.

Discussion also involved expressions of optimism about the shift in values over the last 20 years towards greater inclusion. However, translating this into whole school developments was dependent, it was asserted, on developing the right kind of school ethos. This led into discussions about what we meant by inclusion and whether it had any limits. There were calls for clarity in defining inclusion, for example in relation to an inclusive National Curriculum. Someone asserted that disapplication of the National Curriculum was an offence to curriculum entitlement. One suggestion was that inclusion had to be strategic, progressive and owned locally. But this did not address the question of the limits to inclusion. How far, it was asked, can schools be inclusive without fearing damage to other children? Some children, it was argued, are regarded in schools as 'not desirable' to include.

Concluding comments

One of the main concluding themes of the Policy Seminar was that we need to carry on talking about inclusion. We need to continue to scrutinise our assumptions about inclusion. For some participants inclusion was about all children. It represented a broader gaze, a cultural commitment, not just a limited gaze on children with disabilities and difficulties. The issue was presented as one of making the education system, in its current form, compatible with inclusive values. To realise these values required changing the context of schooling. For others, the idea of setting inclusion targets for schools made them wince. Children, it was argued, go to school to receive a high quality education. Inclusion from this perspective is one amongst several guiding values to which we should be committed in education. The counter argument was that education was not just an individual matter, it was about learning to live together as a group. This prompted some people to want to say more about inclusion, especially at a time when there is a denial of inclusive values and practices. In this perspective, schools have a critical role in society as part of wider social policies. In an attempt to resolve this difference between individual and social perspectives, it was asserted that the best schools are inclusive ones. Was inclusion not about good education? Not so, was the response.

51

Inclusion is not at the heart of education. The essence is more about excellence in teaching and learning, with inclusion part of this. In another attempt to resolve the tension, it was argued that inclusion is a developmental process. Children in special settings, like special units or classes, though in separate provision, could be enabled to participate in a school's mainstream activities. But, as another participant pointed out, the policy discussions had not covered transformational processes. Was a school striving for GCSE results a good place for children with difficulties in learning? Were there tensions between going for higher standards and establishing a school as a good place for all children? In concluding the seminar it was noted that these debates let the focus slip from practical reviews and developments. The seminar ended with a call for continuing to maintain a dual focus on both the practicalities of inclusive developments and the debates about values, concepts and commitments.